Athletics

Bernie Blackall

Heinemann
LIBRARY

First published in Great Britain by Heinemann Library,
Halley Court, Jordan Hill, Oxford OX2 8EJ,
a division of Reed Educational & Professional Publishing Ltd.

02 01 00 99 98
10 9 8 7 6 5 4 3 2 1

Series cover and text design by Karen Young
Paged by Jo Pritchard
Cover by Smarty-pants Design
Edited by Jane Pearson
Illustrations by Xiangyi Mo and Jingwen Wang
Production by Alexandra Tannock
Printed in Malaysia by Times Offset (M) Sdn. Bhd.

ISBN 0431 08499 8.

British Library
Cataloguing in Publication data:

Blackall, Bernie.
    Athletics. - (Top Sport)
    1. Athletics – Juvenile literature.
    I. Title
    796.4'2

Acknowledgements
The publisher would like to thank: Rebel Sport, Prahran; students
from Armadale Primary School – Robert Klein, Nicola Murdock,
Khoa Nguyen, Mimosa Rizzo, Andrew Scott, Charlotte Scheck-
Shaw, Zheng Yu; Malerie Weston, Neil Fowler and Ian Scott for
their help with this book.

Photographs supplied by:
The Little Athletics Association of Australia, pages 4, 5, 13, 14, 17,
19, 21, 22, 24, 25, 27; Malcolm Cross, page 10; Wies Fajzullin,
pages 11, 16; Sport The Library, page 15; Ancient Art &
Architecture Museum, pages 8, 9; Empics, pages 6, 7.

Contents

About athletics

There are several sports or events that make up athletics. These are divided into two areas – track events and field events. Track events are mainly running events that are held on a track around the outside of the field. Field events involve throwing and jumping and are held in special areas inside the track.

Athletics events developed from ancient sports. Today they are a major part of the Olympic Games where competitors strive to run fastest, throw farthest, and jump highest or longest.

Track events

Sprints:
100 m, 200 m, 400 m
Middle distance:
800 m and 1500 m
Long distance:
5 000 m and 10 000 m
Hurdles:
100 m (women), 110 m (men),
400 m (men and women)
Race walks:
10 km (women),
20 km (men), 50 km (men)
Relays:
4 x 100 m, 4 x 400 m
Marathon:
42.195 km
Steeplechase:
3000 m (men)

Field events

Throwing events:
Javelin
Discus
Shot put
Hammer
Jumping events:
Long jump
High jump
Triple jump
Pole vault

Athletic tracks are usually eight lanes wide and 400 metres long, stretching around the outside of a grassy field. They usually have a synthetic weatherproof surface.

Safety first

To participate safely you will need to listen carefully to your coaches and officials, and observe the safety requirements closely – especially for the throwing events!

British highlights

Great Britain has been one of the leading nations in world athletics for many years. Britain has won medals for athletics at every one of the modern Olympic Games.

Sprinting

Harold Abrahams was the first British Olympic champion in sprinting. He won the 100m final at the 1924 Games in Paris. The British 100m gold did not come until 1980 when Alan Wells from Scotland triumphed in Moscow. Since then, sprinting has boomed with Linford Christie winning Olympic and World Championships and equalling the World Record. Colin Jackson became World Record-holder for the 100m hurdles.

Over the longer sprint distance of 400m Britain has also achieved great success. Roger Black led the British 4 x 400m relay team to the Olympic silver medal in Atlanta. In the 400m hurdles, Sally Gunnell set the World Record and won both World Championship and Olympic gold.

Middle distance

In 1954 Roger Bannister became the first man to run a mile in under four minutes. Running on a cinder track in Oxford, Bannister was helped by two other British runners, Chataway and Brasher, to break what then seemed an impossible barrier.

During the 1980s Britain produced three of the best middle-distance runners the world has ever seen. Steve Ovett, Sebastian Coe and Steve Cram won all the major championships and set a series of World Records from 800m to the mile. Kelly Holmes has continued the tradition of British middle-distance running, winning World Championship medals for both 800 and 1500m.

Kelly Holmes is the latest in a long line of great British middle-distance runners. She has won medals at both World Championships and Olympic Games.

Field events

In the 1960s, Mary Rand and Lynn Davies both achieved success in the long jump event and set British records which lasted for nearly 20 years. In 1995, Jonathan Edwards became the first man to triple-jump over 18m, and won the World Championship gold and Olympic silver in Atlanta in 1996.

Through the 1980s Tessa Sanderson and Fatima Whitbread were among the world's leading javelin throwers setting World Records and taking gold at major games. In the 1990s Steve Backley has taken centre stage setting the World Record and winning the gold medal at the World Championships and silver in the Olympics in Atlanta.

Multi events

Daley Thompson was considered to be the greatest athlete of his time competing in the decathlon event. He won gold at both the 1980 and 1984 Olympics and set the World Record in the process. In 1994, Denise Lewis won the Commonwealth gold medal for the heptathlon and followed this with a silver in the 1996 Olympics in Atlanta.

Britain's men's 4x400m relay team are among the best in the world. They won the silver medal in the Atlanta Olympics.

Colin Jackson flies fast and low over the hurdle.

History of athletics

Athletics is one of the oldest sports. It can be traced back more than 3000 years to running races in Greece. Ancient art from many cultures shows running events and activities such as **javelin**, **discus** and jumping. These events probably developed from hunting and warfare training.

The Ancient Olympics

Athletics were part of the ancient Olympic Games which were held at Olympia in Greece. The first recorded Olympic champion was Coroelous, a cook from Elis in Greece. He won the sprint race at the Games in 776 BC. At this time, the Olympic Games consisted of only one event – a race over the length of the stadium (about 211 metres). Later, longer races and other events including javelin, discus and long jump were added. Athletics remained part of the games for over 1000 years until the last ancient Olympics in AD 303.

A medal from the ancient Olympic Games

The marathon

The **marathon** takes its name from Greek legend. When the Greeks defeated the Persians at the Battle of Marathon, Pheidippides, a messenger, ran 41.83 kilometres to Athens to announce the news. He collapsed and died soon after arriving.

At the first Modern Olympic Games, athletes raced over the same course that Pheidippides had run. The event became known as the marathon. At the London Olympics in 1908 the distance of the marathon was lengthened by 365 metres to allow the British King to watch the end of the race from the comfort of his box in the stadium.

This ancient Greek urn from the 4th century BC depicts a running race.

The Modern Olympics

Some of the first 'modern' athletics competitions were organised as part of soldiers' training. Then in 1896, the French Baron, Pierre du Coubertin, revived the Olympics in Athens – athletics was again part of the games. Today the Olympics is the most important international athletics competition.

Women were excluded from the Ancient Olympic Games, both as competitors and as spectators.

Shot put

The shot put event developed from the ancient sport of stone throwing. It was developed by British military sports groups who used cannon balls, or 'shots', in throwing competitions. Shot put, using a standard metal shot, was included in the Olympics at the first Modern Olympic Games in 1896.

The track Sprints

Sprints are the shortest and fastest races. They are run over distances of 100 metres, 200 metres and 400 metres. Competitors run the entire distance as fast as they can and must stay in their own lanes.

The sprint start

Every fraction of a second counts in a sprint race so it is crucial to get off to a fast start. There are two ways to start a sprint race. The standing start is used by young children. The crouch start is used by older children and senior athletes. **Starting blocks** are usually used for crouch starts as they help athletes get the maximum drive and acceleration. The blocks are placed two foot lengths behind the starting line.

From the crouch start, try to move quickly and smoothly into the running action.

The race starter calls three commands: 'On your marks', 'Set', 'Go'.

On your marks

Put your thumbs and first fingers on the starting line so that your hands make arches. Put your feet on the blocks so that your weight is on the balls of your feet. Your front knee should be level with your elbows.

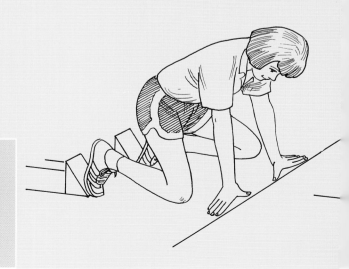

Running shoes

It is important to wear a good pair of shoes that support your feet as you run. Senior athletes and many older children wear light-weight shoes with spikes for extra grip.

The running action

After starting powerfully, it is important to move quickly into a strong running action.

Focus your eyes on a point and hold your head steady. Keep your body relaxed and lift your knees high to achieve long strides. Your hips should be high and your body leaning slightly forward. Move your arms backwards and forwards, keeping your elbows bent at about a 90° angle. This arm movement is important for keeping your balance as you run.

The running action

Set

Lift your hips up. Keep your arms straight and lift your head to look at the track one metre ahead. Keep your shoulders forward and most of your weight on your fingers ready to spring into action.

Go

Push forward powerfully. Pump your arms hard to help you accelerate into the sprint.

The track
Relays

Relays involve teams of four runners aiming to carry a **baton** from the start to the finish as quickly as possible. The runners begin the relay positioned at intervals around the track. The first runner from each team starts the race carrying the baton, which is passed from team member to team member as quickly as possible without slowing down at the changeover until the last runner crosses the finish line. There are two relay race distances: 4 x 100 metres and 4 x 400 metres. In the 4 x 100 metres relay, all runners must stay in their own lanes. In the 4 x 400 metres relays, runners can move out of their lanes to the shorter inner lane after the first 500 metres.

Positions for a 4 x 100 metres relay race

As the incoming runner reaches the **acceleration zone** he or she shouts 'Go'. The receiver then races away and the baton is passed at top speed in the **changeover zone**. Smooth baton changes will ensure your team's best result.

Staggered starts and changeover zones ensure that all teams complete the same distance on the curved track.

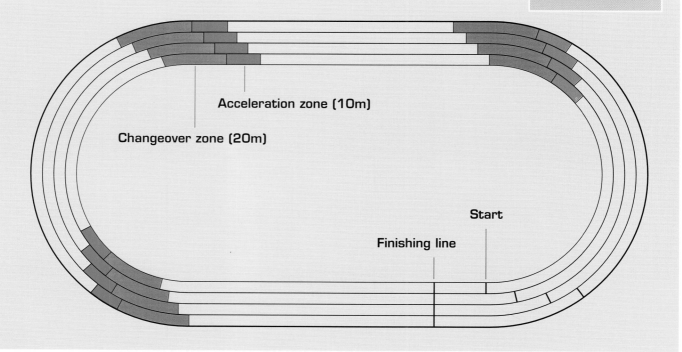

Acceleration zone (10m)

Changeover zone (20m)

Start

Finishing line

Passing the baton

As the incoming runner approaches, the receiver takes off. If the runner is carrying the baton in the right hand, the receiver holds his or her left hand outstretched behind. The palm should face upwards and the thumb and fingers should form a 'V'. The incoming runner passes the baton down into the hand of the receiver. The new runner will sprint his or her leg of the race, keeping the baton in the same hand; the baton is passed alternatively from the right hand of one runner to the left hand of the next, and so on.

It is important not to look back as you receive the baton as this will slow you down.

Practise your baton changes slowly at first. Then, when you have mastered the technique, add speed for a fast, smooth changeover.

The changeover

The incoming runner passes the baton down into the open palm of the receiving runner.

The track
Hurdles

Hurdles is a sprint race where the runners clear obstacles, called hurdles. It is important to move smoothly over the hurdles in a way that slows you down as little as possible. Keep low and avoid 'jumping' as that extra height means wasted time.

You can take an odd number of strides between hurdles to lead with the same leg each time, or take an even number strides and lead with alternate legs.

The hurdle action

Try to establish a rhythm as you 'run' over the hurdles.

As you approach the hurdle, imagine you are putting your knee under your chin. Aim your lead leg high, keeping it pointing straight ahead.

Dip your body forward as you pass over the hurdle. Push the arm opposite your lead leg forward.

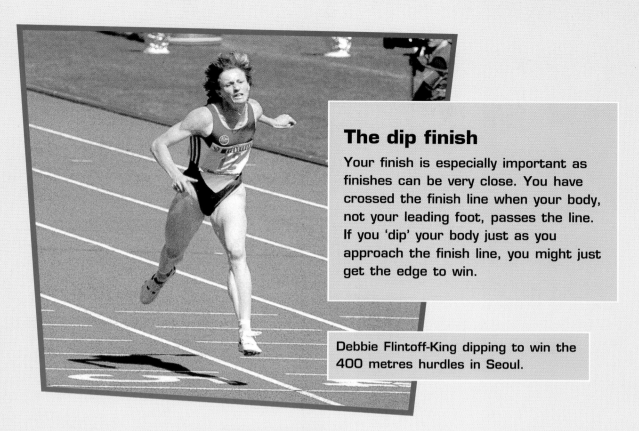

The dip finish

Your finish is especially important as finishes can be very close. You have crossed the finish line when your body, not your leading foot, passes the line. If you 'dip' your body just as you approach the finish line, you might just get the edge to win.

Debbie Flintoff-King dipping to win the 400 metres hurdles in Seoul.

If you accidentally knock a hurdle you will not be disqualified. However knocking a hurdle will throw you off balance and slow you down.

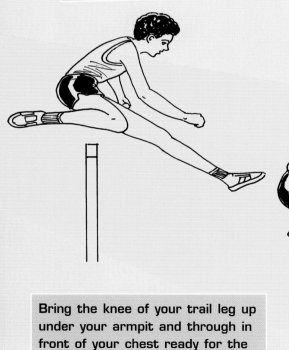

Bring the knee of your trail leg up under your armpit and through in front of your chest ready for the next stride.

Bring your trail leg over to the side and keep your body low over the hurdle to clear it at maximum speed.

The track
Distance running

Middle and long distance running events require good fitness and stamina. The style of running and the rules for these events are different from those of the sprints.

The starter's calls for distance events are 'On your marks' and 'Go' (there is no 'Set'). The starting line is curved and runners don't use starting blocks. Competitors don't stay in individual lanes, but move across to the inside of the track soon after the start.

The distance running action is geared for endurance with an upright body position and less pronounced arm and leg movements than those used for sprinting.

Once the race starts, move to the inside of the track, as this is the shortest course to the finish. Move quickly to avoid ending up at the back of the field, but be careful not to bump or trip other runners. Try to keep in touch with the leaders but pace yourself so that as the over-ambitious runners drop back, you are in a strong position.

Always be prepared for a sprint to the finish line. Run hard right across the line – don't slow up for the last few steps.

The track
Race walking

Walking is an athletics sport. Competitors walk as fast as they can. There are rules that must be followed to make sure no one breaks into a run. You must always have at least one foot on the ground – your back foot must not leave the ground until the front one touches it. As each foot touches the ground, your leg should straighten briefly.

Keep your body upright. Bend your arms and swing them forward and across your chest to neck height. This will help to drive you forwards.

Rotate your hips slightly before your foot lands to lengthen your stride. Place each foot down heel first and straighten your knee soon after contact.

The field
Javelin

Javelin is a throwing event. The javelin itself is a spear-shaped object, about 2.5 metres long with a metal point. Competitors aim to throw it as far as possible so that the point touches the ground first when it lands.

The grip

There are two basic grips for throwing the javelin – for each one, place your hand towards the back of the grip area and keep your palm upwards. Practise using each grip and then choose the one you find more comfortable.

The throw

As a beginner, practise in a standing position. Once you have perfected the throw, add a few steps for a run-up. Build up gradually to speed that will add force to your throw.

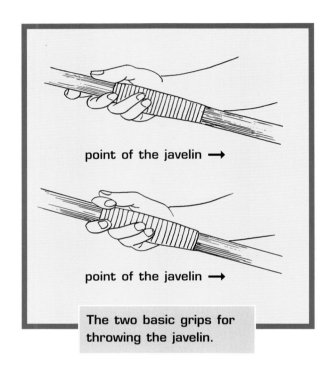

point of the javelin →

point of the javelin →

The two basic grips for throwing the javelin.

Safety

It is very important to follow safety rules when competing in or practising javelin throwing. Stand well clear of anyone throwing a javelin. Never throw a javelin if anyone is in or near the throwing area.

Start your run-up with the javelin at ear level, parallel to the ground.

Raise your arm and take the javelin back as you begin to turn side on.

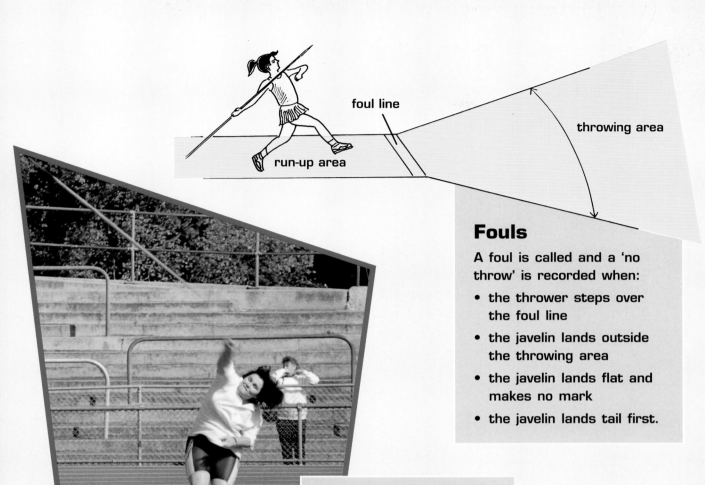

foul line

throwing area

run-up area

Fouls

A foul is called and a 'no throw' is recorded when:

- the thrower steps over the foul line
- the javelin lands outside the throwing area
- the javelin lands flat and makes no mark
- the javelin lands tail first.

As you release the javelin your weight should be on the foot opposite your throwing arm.

Lift your other elbow high and take a long stride.

Drive the javelin forwards, leading with your elbow. Push your other arm back and around.

Flick the javelin with your fingers as you release it. Be careful not to step over the foul line.

The field
Discus

The **discus** is an almost flat disc. Competitors throw it from a metal-rimmed concrete circle as far as possible into the **throwing area**. There is no run-up for discus – you must generate as much momentum as possible while remaining in the **throwing circle**. Competitors must enter and leave from the back half of the throwing circle. Usually each competitor has three throws and the best one is recorded.

The discus must land in the throwing area which makes a 40° arc from the centre of the throwing circle.

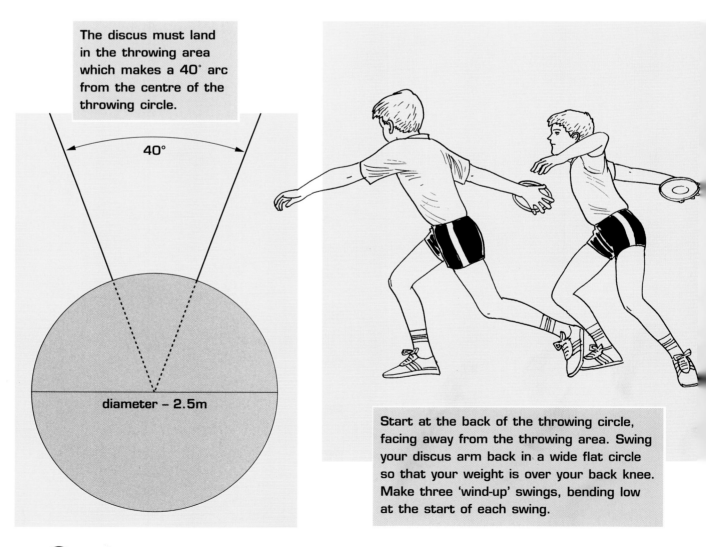

40°

diameter – 2.5m

Start at the back of the throwing circle, facing away from the throwing area. Swing your discus arm back in a wide flat circle so that your weight is over your back knee. Make three 'wind-up' swings, bending low at the start of each swing.

The grip

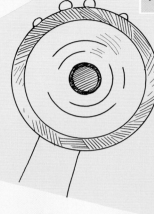

Hold the discus flat against your palm and wrist. Spread your fingers so that they reach just over the rim. Your thumb should rest across the top for balance.

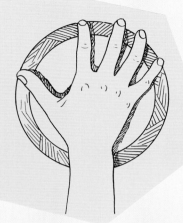

As you prepare to throw, concentrate hard, keeping your eyes on the discus.

Turn your back leg, hips and then your shoulders as you swing around and up, stretching onto your toes and looking out in the direction you will throw.

At the end of the final swing, release the discus off your index finger so that it spins in a clockwise direction out into the throwing area.

The field
Shot put

The **shot put** event involves throwing, or putting, a heavy ball of metal, called a shot, from the throwing circle into the throwing area. Putting the shot requires a complete body movement. The power starts in your legs and moves through your body to your arms and fingers and then finally the shot. Start with the standing throw shown below. Then, once you have mastered it, begin the procedure at the back of the throwing circle and side-skip forward to add momentum to your throw.

You must enter and leave the throwing circle from the back half.

The standing throw

Stand side-on. Place the shot under your chin and close to your neck. Keep your elbow high.

Shift your weight onto your back leg and bend down to it, ready to spring up and around.

Thrust your leading shoulder forward, pushing powerfully off your back leg to turn towards the throwing area.

No part of your body may touch the ground outside the circle during your put. Your toe may touch the inside of the **stop board** but not the top of it. The shot must land in the throwing area.

 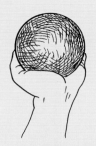

The grip

Hold the shot at the base of your fingers so that three fingers are behind, and your thumb and small finger are on either side. Keep your wrist bent back.

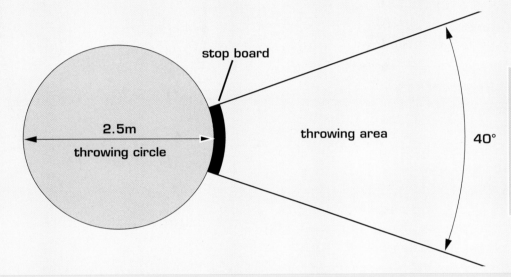

stop board

2.5m
throwing circle

throwing area

40°

The shot is 'put' from a concrete throwing circle which is 2.5 metres in diameter. At the front of this circle is a raised stop board, 10 centimetres high.

Move your weight onto your front foot as you push the shot upwards and forwards.

Follow through powerfully – be careful to stay inside the throwing circle!

The field
Long jump and triple jump

Competitors in **long jump** and **triple jump** aim to cover the greatest horizontal distance. The same jumping pit can be used for both jumps, and both have the same take-off rule. You can take off from on or behind the **take-off board** but if any part of your foot is over it, a 'no jump' results.

The jumps are measured from the part of the mark left in the sand nearest the take-off board. Falling back will result in a shorter jump, so try to bend your knees and push your hips and shoulders forward as you land. Competitors usually make three jumps each – the best one is recorded.

The take off

Your longest jump will be achieved with a fast run-up. When you take off, aim to jump upwards as well as forwards with a strong spring from your take-off foot.

Long jump

Long jump

Long jump is a single jump from the take-off board into the pit.

Lift your leading knee high as you take off. Stretch your leg forwards and push your arms high into the air.

Triple jump

Triple jump is often called 'hop, step and jump' because that's what it involves.

Practise getting the actions right before you add a fast run-up. Speak through the movement as you practise. Once you have the actions right, concentrate on keeping your hips high, gathering speed and increasing the distance you cover in each phase.

Each phase of the triple jump should be a similar length. Ask a friend to mark your landings and then measure them.

For the hop, land on the same foot you took off from.

Then take a step to land on the other foot.

Spring off to jump, landing in the pit with both feet together.

Push your arms back to help thrust your body forward. As you land, bring your arms forward to help stop you from falling back.

The field
High jump

High jump competitors aim to jump the greatest vertical distance. They jump over a bar which is raised a little higher after each round. Competitors who fail to clear a height are knocked out and their best clear jump is recorded. The winner is the one who clears the greatest height.

There are two jumping techniques. The **Fosbury flop** will take you higher, but the **scissor action** is simpler for beginners.

The scissor action

Set the bar at a height you think you can clear. Stand about 5 metres from the bar. Run up to the bar in a curved path so that you approach it side-on. Kick your legs up and over the bar.

The scissor jump

Kick the leg nearest the bar up and over.

Raise your arms for extra lift as your other leg follows.

Land on your bottom on the crash mat.

The Fosbury flop

The Fosbury flop is the most effective method of high jumping. Start with the bar set low and raise it as you improve the technique.

You can try different approach lengths and curves to find the best ones for you. Use your take-off foot, your kicking leg and your arms to create as much spring as possible for your maximum jump height.

Keep your feet up as your body clears the bar – just a small knock will cause the bar to fall.

The Fosbury flop

Approach the bar in the same way as for the scissor jump. As you take off, start to do a scissor jump, but with your leading leg bent.

Turn your shoulders so that your back faces the bar and arch your back to clear the bar.

Land on the mat on your back.

Getting ready

You should always warm up your muscles and stretch before training or competing to prepare your body for activity and to help avoid injury.

Inner thigh stretch
Stand with your feet wide apart and toes pointing forwards. Rest your hands on one thigh and bend that knee. Keep your back straight. Hold the stretch for a few seconds and then slowly stand up and stretch to the other side.

Star jumps
Stand with your feet together and arms by your side, Jump and land with your feet apart and arms outstretched. Jump back to the start position. Repeat about 15 times.

Arm circles
Stretch your arms up above your head and then take them around in circles.

Push-ups

Lie face down on the ground with your hands below your shoulders and toes tucked under. Keep your body straight and push up with your arms. (You can also do push ups with your knees on the ground.) Repeat 10 times.

Sit-ups

Lie on your back with your knees bent and hands behind your head. Keep your feet on the ground and sit up. Slowly lie down again. Repeat 10 times.

Hurdle stretch

Sit with one leg bent to the side and stretch forward to the other leg. Hold the stretch for a few seconds. Then change position and stretch the other side.

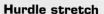

Side bends

Stand with your feet shoulder-width apart and your arms stretched above your head. Bend sideways from the hips. Make sure you don't lean forwards or backwards as you bend. Straighten up and then bend to the other side.

Taking it further

For more information about British athletics contact:-

The British Athletics Federation
Edgebaston House
3 Duchess Place
Birmingham B16 8NM
☎ 0121 440 5000

South East
Richard Simmons
Crystal Palace National Sports Centre
Norwood
London SE19 2BB
☎ 0181 776 6368

West
Dave Lease
22 Ludmead Road
Corsham
Wiltshire SN13 9AS
☎ 01249 713896

North West
Peter Warden
North West Coaching Office
37 St Peter's Street
Preston
Lancashire PR1 7BS
☎ 01772 254318

Scotland
Scottish Athletics Federation
Caledonian House
South Gyle
Edinburgh EH12 9DQ
☎ 0131 317 7320

Wales
Phil Banning
Athletics Association of Wales
Morfa Stadium
Landore
Swansea
West Glamorgan SA1 7DF
☎ 01792 463177

Northern Ireland
Brian Hall
Mary Peters Track
Athletics House
Old Coach Road
Belfast
☎ 01232 602707

Further reading

Successful Sports: Athlectics, Tony Ward, Heinemann Library, Oxford, 1995
Olympic Library: Track, Tony Ward, Heinemann Library, Oxford, 1996
Olympic Library: Field, Tony Ward, Heinemann Library, Oxford, 1996

Glossary

acceleration zone an area of the track where relay runners may begin running before receiving the baton.

baton a hollow tube that is passed from one runner to the next in relay races.

changeover zone an area of the track where the baton must be passed from one relay runner to the next.

discus a metal-weighted disc. Discus is a field event.

Fosbury flop the most effective technique for clearing the high jump bar.

high jump an athletics event where competitors aim to clear a horizontal bar.

hurdles a race where runners clear a series of obstacles (also known as hurdles).

javelin a spear-like object which is thrown. Javelin is a field event.

long jump a horizontal jumping event.

race walking events where competitors walk. One foot must be touching the track at all times.

relay a team running event where a baton is passed from runner to runner.

scissor action a technique for clearing the high jump bar, usually used by beginners.

shot put an field event where a metal ball (shot) is thrown (put).

sprint a short race where competitors cover the whole distance at top speed.

starting blocks blocks used for sprint starts to give maximum push-off.

stop board a curved piece of wood at the front edge of the shot put throwing circle for discus and shot put events. Competitors must not step over the stop board.

take-off board a wooden board at the end of the long jump or triple jump run up. Competitors take off from on or behind the take-off board.

throwing area area that the javelin, discus or shot put must land in for these events.

throwing circle concrete circle from which the shot put and discus events take place.

triple jump a jump sequence involving a hop, a step and a jump.

Index